South American Animals

Sloths

ABDO
Publishing Company

Big
Buddy BOOKS
South American
Animals

by Julie Murray

VISIT US AT

www.abdopublishing.com

Published by ABDO Publishing Company, PO Box 398166, Minneapolis, Minnesota 55439.

Printed in the United States of America, North Mankato, Minnesota.
092013
012014

 PRINTED ON RECYCLED PAPER

Coordinating Series Editor: Rochelle Baltzer
Editor: Marcia Zappa
Contributing Editors: Megan M. Gunderson, Bridget O'Brien, Sarah Tieck
Graphic Design: Maria Hosley
Cover Photograph: *Glow Images*: Wayne Lynch.
Interior Photographs/Illustrations: *Glow Images*: Barrett & MacKay (p. 25), Fabian Fischer (p. 17), Thomas
    Haupt (p. 25), Ivan Kuzmin (p. 29), Gerard Lacz (p. 11), Wayne Lynch (pp. 7, 13, 27), SuperStock (p. 19);
    iStockphoto: ©iStockphoto.com/hotshotsworldwide (p. 21), ©iStockphoto.com/kjorgen (p. 9), ©iStockphoto.
    com/milehightraveler (p. 5), ©iStockphoto.com/JohanSjolander (p. 4), ©iStockphoto.com/vilainecrevette (p. 11);
    Minden Pictures: © Suzi Eszterhas (p. 23), © Michael_Patricia Fogden (pp. 15, 17); *Shutterstock*: Ammit Jack
    (p. 4), BMJ (p. 21), Tami Freed (p. 13), Pichugin Dmitry (p. 8), Luiz Rocha (p. 9), Toniflap (p. 9).

Library of Congress Cataloging-in-Publication Data

Murray, Julie, 1969- author.
  Sloths / Julie Murray.
     pages cm. -- (South American animals)
  Audience: 7 to 11.
  ISBN 978-1-62403-193-9
  1. Sloths--Juvenile literature. I. Title.
  QL737.E2M87 2014
  599.3'13--dc23
                        2013025486

Contents

Amazing South American Animals 4

Sloth Territory 6

Welcome to South America! 8

Take a Closer Look 10

Life in Trees 14

Slow and Safe. 18

Mealtime 22

Baby Sloths 26

Survivors 28

Wow! I'll bet you never knew... 30

Important Words 31

Web Sites 31

Index 32

Long ago, nearly all land on Earth was one big mass. About 200 million years ago, the land began to break into **continents**. One of these is South America.

Sloths are known for moving slowly through their treetop homes.

South America includes several countries and cultures. It is known for its rain forests and interesting animals. One of these animals is the sloth.

Sloth Territory

The two main types of sloths are two-toed sloths and three-toed sloths. Both live in northern South America and Central America. Central America is the southern part of North America.

Sloths live in **tropical** rain forests. These areas are warm, wet, and thick with plants.

Uncovered!
Sloths are related to armadillos and anteaters.

Sloth Territory

Sloths spend almost their entire lives in trees.

Welcome to South America!

If you took a trip to where sloths live, you might find…

SOUTH

ACIFIC

CEAN

SOU

Strait of Magellan

ape Horn

…warm weather.

About three-quarters of South America is in the tropics. This area of earth is near the equator. That makes the weather there warm year-round!

...plants and trees.

South America is home to the world's largest tropical rain forest. The Amazon has more types of plants than anywhere else in the world! This includes many trees that sloths live in, such as cecropia trees.

...large cities.

More than two-thirds of the people in South America live in cities. Some South American cities are very large. These include São Paulo and Rio de Janeiro (*left*) in Brazil and Buenos Aires (*below*) in Argentina. But, sloths live in less populated areas.

9

Take a Closer Look

Three-toed sloths look like they are always smiling! This is caused by the colors of the fur on their faces.

Sloths have rounded bodies and long **limbs**. Three-toed sloths have short tails that are often hidden by fur. Two-toed sloths have very short tails or none at all. A sloth's flat face has two round eyes, a broad nose, and a thin mouth.

Sloths have long, **shaggy** fur. It is tan, brown, or gray.

Uncovered!
Three-toed sloths have extra neck bones. This allows them to turn their heads almost all the way around!

Sloths spend much of their time hanging below tree branches. So, their fur grows from their bellies toward their backs.

Being light helps sloths live in trees. To reach food, they climb on thin branches that can't hold heavier animals.

Adult sloths are 18 to 30 inches (46 to 76 cm) long. They weigh 6.5 to 20 pounds (3 to 9 kg). This is light compared to other animals of the same size.

All sloths have three sharp claws on each back **limb**. Two-toed sloths have two claws on each front limb. Three-toed sloths have three claws on each front limb. A sloth's claws are 3 to 4 inches (8 to 10 cm) long.

Sloths may not move well on the ground, but they are strong swimmers!

17

Slow and Safe

Sloths are known for being slow movers. They move through trees by walking **limb**-over-limb underneath branches.

Being slow helps keep sloths safe. Predators such as jaguars and harpy eagles use their sharp eyes to find food. But, sloths sleep so much and move so slowly that predators often don't notice them!

Uncovered!
A sloth's other predators include hawks, boas, anacondas, large cats, and humans.

Sloths are the slowest mammals in the world! Two-toed sloths (*above*) move slightly faster than three-toed sloths.

Many sloths have tiny plants called algae (AL-jee) growing on their fur. This makes their fur look green. It helps them hide even better in their treetop homes!

If a sloth faces a predator, it can't easily escape. So, it bites, hisses, shrieks, and swipes with its sharp claws!

Sloths lick the algae on their fur for food.

Sloths are in the most danger of being attacked on the ground.

Mealtime

Sloths eat many different foods found in their treetop homes. They mostly eat leaves. But, sloths also eat fruit, buds, and twigs. Sometimes, they eat bugs or small lizards.

Sloths get almost all of the water they need from the plants they eat.

The leaves that sloths eat are hard to **digest**. So, sloths have special stomachs with many parts. Food moves slowly through a sloth's stomach.

Leaves don't provide sloths with much **energy**. So, sloths have a slow metabolism. This means they use the energy from their food slowly over time. And sloths have low body temperatures. This helps them save energy.

It may take a month for a sloth to digest a meal! For a human, this only takes a few days.

Because sloths save energy, they don't need to eat much.

Baby Sloths

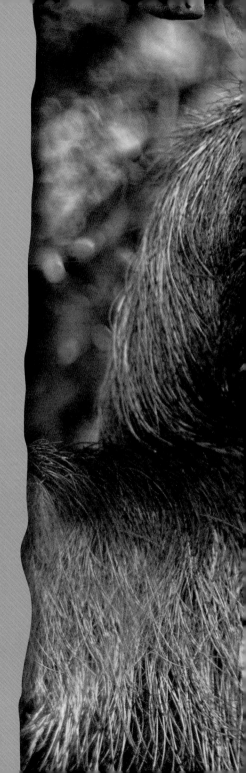

Sloths are **mammals**. Females usually have one baby at a time. A newborn sloth often weighs less than one pound (0.5 kg). It drinks its mother's milk and grows.

At first, a baby sloth clings to its mother's belly. Later, it begins to follow her through the treetops. After six months to two years, it is ready to live on its own.

A baby sloth often continues to ride on its mother's belly even after it stops drinking her milk.

Survivors

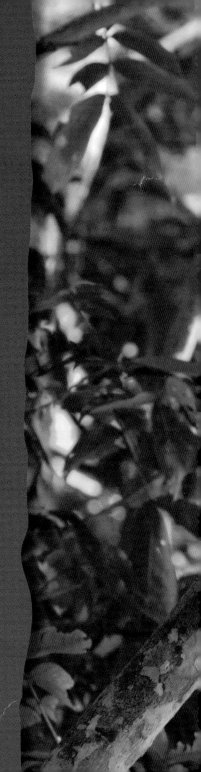

Life in South America isn't easy for sloths. Predators, including humans, hunt them. New buildings and farms take over their **habitats**. And, accidents with power lines and roads harm them.

Still, sloths **survive**. People work to make sure they have safe areas to live freely. Sloths help make South America an amazing place!

In the wild, sloths live for 10 to 20 years.

Uncovered!
Some types of sloths are endangered. This means they are in danger of dying out.

29

Wow!

I'll bet you never knew...

...that three-toed sloths can only live in the wild. They can't **survive** in zoos or as pets.

...that October 20 is International Sloth Day!

...that long ago, giant ground sloths lived in the United States. Some grew as large as elephants! They died out about 10,000 years ago.

...that a sloth may continue hanging from a tree even after it dies. That's because its claws allow it to hang with such little effort!

Important Words

continent one of Earth's seven main land areas.

culture (KUHL-chuhr) the arts, beliefs, and ways of life of a group of people.

digest (deye-JEHST) to break down food into parts small enough for the body to use.

energy (EH-nuhr-jee) the power or ability to do things.

habitat a place where a living thing is naturally found.

limb (LIHM) an arm, leg, or wing.

mammal a member of a group of living beings. Mammals make milk to feed their babies and usually have hair or fur on their skin.

mate to join as a couple in order to reproduce, or have babies. A mate is a partner to join with in order to reproduce.

shaggy made up of long, tangled hair or fur.

survive to continue to live or exist.

tropical of or relating to parts of the world where temperatures are warm and the air is moist all the time.

Web Sites

To learn more about sloths, visit ABDO Publishing Company online. Web sites about sloths are featured on our Book Links page. These links are routinely monitored and updated to provide the most current information available.

www.abdopublishing.com

Index

Amazon rain forest **9**

Argentina **9**

babies **14, 26, 27**

body **10, 11, 12, 16, 18, 24, 26, 27**

Brazil **9**

Central America **6**

claws **12, 13, 14, 15, 16, 20, 30**

communication **14**

dangers **18, 20, 21, 28**

eating habits **12, 14, 21, 22, 23, 24, 25, 26, 27**

fur **10, 11, 20, 21**

habitat **5, 6, 9, 20, 22, 28**

mammals **19, 26**

mating **14**

moving **5, 16, 17, 18, 19**

predators **18, 20, 28**

size **12, 13, 26, 30**

South America **4, 5, 6, 8, 9, 28**

three-toed sloths **6, 10, 12, 13, 19, 30**

two-toed sloths **6, 10, 12, 13, 19**

weather **6, 8**